MUSIC THROUGHOUT HISTORY™

HAYDN'S WORLD

JAMES R. NORTON

rosen publishing's
rosen central®

New York

To Mark Messer, who tried valiantly over the course of four years to teach me how to play the cello

Published in 2008 by The Rosen Publishing Group, Inc.
29 East 21st Street, New York, NY 10010

First Edition

Library of Congress Cataloging-in-Publication Data

Norton, James R.
Haydn's world/James R. Norton.—1st ed.
    p. cm.—(Music throughout history)
Includes bibliographical references (p.   ) and index.
ISBN-13: 978-1-4042-0727-1
ISBN-10: 1-4042-0727-9
1. Haydn, Joseph, 1732–1809—Juvenile literature.
2. Composers—Austria—Biography—Juvenile literature.
I. Title.
ML3930.H3N67 2008
780.92—dc22 [B]
                                                    2007000907

Manufactured in the United States of America

On the cover: An eighteenth-century portrait of Joseph Haydn.

CONTENTS

Joseph Haydn

The composer Joseph Haydn rose from humble beginnings to

INTRODUCTION

When Joseph Haydn wrote, "I was forced to become original," in the late eighteenth century, he was referring to the artistic isolation that he experienced as a court musician. Cut off from his big-city peers, the composer did much of his best work in relative solitude on a country estate near the modern-day border between Austria and Hungary. However, few who study the composer's remarkable musical accomplishments can doubt that Haydn would have developed a truly original voice, regardless of where he settled.

Haydn's story is one of the great rags-to-riches tales in the history of music. From a talented country boy in tattered clothes who fought for table scraps, Haydn rose to become one of the most notable court musicians of his day. He also became the central figure of one of the most productive and influential times in musical history: the Classical period.

Today, "classical music" is a general term that includes multiple styles of music, spanning many centuries up to the present. But the Classical period specifically spans the years between 1730 and 1820, not coincidentally overlapping almost precisely with Haydn's life.

Just as Haydn began his career, the Baroque era of music had begun to fade. Ornamented, overly complicated music was going out of style, and Haydn would help lead the charge toward clearer divisions between parts, brighter contrasts, and a preference for simplicity. Moreover, changes in the intellectual and social structure of Europe had begun to create a new clarity in science, politics, and art. Thinkers such as Isaac Newton (1642–1727) and Francis Bacon (1561–1626) had touched off a revolution in science. The writings of philosophers such as John Locke (1632–1704) and Jean-Jacques Rousseau (1712–1778) would help to start political revolutions against monarchs in America and France. Composers such as Haydn and Wolfgang Amadeus Mozart (1756–1791) would begin a revolution in the world of music. All these things were part of a historic shift toward order and reason that was sweeping across western Europe and the Americas.

While the Enlightenment was a movement far bigger than the contributions of any of its associated thinkers and artists, Haydn's contributions were staggeringly large. Before the end of his long career and life, Haydn would lay the underpinnings of the Classical style, helping to create the symphony orchestra as we know it and almost single-handedly forming the concept of the string quartet. Even near the end of his life, Haydn was pushing his art further toward the future. As H. L. Mencken, one of the twentieth century's most influential critics and journalists, declared in the *Baltimore Evening Sun* on November 22, 1916: "Haydn was more than a great composer of music; he was, beyond everything else, a great musical revolutionary."

CHAPTER ONE

The Early Years

Franz Joseph Haydn was born in 1732 in Rohrau, Lower Austria (he became known to his contemporaries simply as Joseph, without the formal "Franz"). Haydn came from humble beginnings: His father, Mathias, was a poor builder of wheels for wagons and carriages. His mother, Anna Maria Koller, was a cook in the Rohrau castle before she married Mathias. Joseph Haydn showed little inclination to follow in his father's footsteps or become a priest, as his mother hoped. Stories say that he displayed an interest in music at an early age, running around playing make-believe violinist, sawing away at his left arm with a stick.

When Haydn was six years old, he was sent away to nearby Hainsburg, where he learned to read and write,

This nineteenth-century painting shows the birthplace of Haydn, in Rohrau (now part of Austria). The young Haydn sometimes scrounged refreshments at concerts in order to stay fed.

and was taught wind and string instruments. In an autobiographical sketch, as quoted by Harold C. Schonberg in *The Lives of the Great Composers*, Haydn wrote: "Our Almighty Father had endowed me with such fertility in music that even in my sixth year I stood up like a man and sang Masses in the church choir and I could play a little on the clavier and violin."

Haydn was talented but not exceptionally so. However, he was good enough to attract the attention of Georg Reutter (1708–1772), the kapellmeister, or music director, of St. Stephen's Cathedral in Vienna, Austria, who was in charge of auditioning and recruiting new choirboys. After an audition, Reutter brought Haydn, then eight years old, to Vienna to serve in the cathedral choir.

Life in Vienna was difficult for Haydn. Schonberg quotes Haydn as recalling that school consisted of:

more floggings than food. Proper teachers I never had. I always started right away with the practical side, first in singing and playing instruments, later in composing. I listened more than I studied, but I heard the finest music in all forms that was to be heard in my time . . . Thus little by little my knowledge and my ability were developed.

Although Haydn remembered having only two lessons from the busy (and quite famous) kapellmeister, there is little doubt that Reutter's music was a major influence on Haydn's career as a composer. Reutter, over the period of his lifetime, wrote more than 500 church compositions. As a choirboy, Haydn must have come to know some of them intimately. Echoes of their style and texture can be heard in Haydn's own sacred music—even in the pieces that he wrote near the end of his life, a half century later.

LEAVING ST. STEPHEN'S

In 1749, Haydn was dismissed from the choir after his voice broke. If one story about Haydn the schoolboy is to be believed, he probably didn't help his situation by lopping off a fellow student's pigtail as a joke.

Haydn was seventeen when he left the choir. His possessions, in total, consisted of three old shirts and a worn coat. To add insult to injury, the star pupil who took his place at the cathedral was his younger brother, Michael (1737–1806). Michael, for whom great things were predicted, did go on to a distinguished career as a

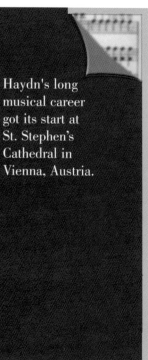

Haydn's long musical career got its start at St. Stephen's Cathedral in Vienna, Austria.

director of the archbishop's orchestra in Salzburg, Austria, and a composer of dozens of symphonies and many sacred works.

Joseph Haydn went through a rough period after leaving St. Stephen's. He scratched out a living by playing at social functions, teaching, and arranging music. He was skilled, but not amazingly good at any particular instrument. In fact, Schonberg quotes Haydn admitting, "I was a wizard on no instrument, but I knew the strength and working of all; I was not a bad clavier player or singer, and could also play a concerto on the violin." This didn't exactly set him apart from other musicians. However, his broad knowledge of instruments and well-balanced sense of how music worked would serve a good basis for a promising future. During this period, he particularly studied the music of Carl Philipp Emanuel Bach (1714–1788) and made headway with his playing. Soon, his reputation grew.

The Kapellmeisters

The word "kapellmeister" is of German origin. It is a combination of the words *kapelle* for "choir" and *meister* for "master." *Kapelle* itself is derived from the Latin word for "chapel," which was, appropriately enough, the center for musical activity during the Middle Ages.

Kapellmeisters, in Haydn's time, were the directors and conductors of orchestras or choirs. It was an important position. A kapellmeister hired and fired musicians, set concert schedules, established orchestra (or choir) policy, and worked with the actual music that the musicians played or sang.

Many great composers spent some or all of their professional years as kapellmeisters. Johann Sebastian Bach (1685–1750) worked from 1717 to 1723 as kapellmeister for the prince of Anhalt-Cöthen, a region of modern-day Germany. George Frideric Handel (1685–1759), another famous composer, served as kapellmeister for Georg, elector of Hanover (1660–1727), who later became King George I of Great Britain. Haydn himself spent many years as kapellmeister to a powerful Hungarian family. The position faded in glory after Haydn's time, however, as society changed and the initiative of individual musicians became more highly valued.

In 1757, Haydn had a breakthrough when he was appointed kapellmeister for Count Ferdinand Maximilian von Morzin. Though he would hold the position for only a few years, it would be a critical stepping stone, as it was through this association that he met his next employer. Three years later, he secured a position as vice kapellmeister to the Esterházys, the richest family in Hungary. The head of the family, Prince Paul Anton Esterházy (1711–1762), loved art and music, and he spent freely from the family's vast fortune, outfitting his palace at Eisenstadt with theaters and concert spaces.

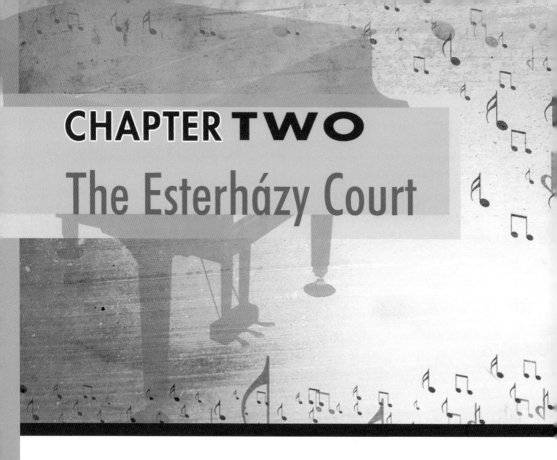

CHAPTER TWO
The Esterházy Court

Being hired by the Esterházys was the most important turning point of Haydn's career. More than just a steady and well-paying job, it was the beginning of the artistic freedom that would help him become one of the greatest composers in the history of music.

Working for the Esterházys—a position he would maintain in one form or another from 1761 until 1790—Haydn soon became familiar with the many advantages and disadvantages of being a court musician. During the first five years on the job, the major disadvantage was a sometimes difficult working relationship with his predecessor, kapellmeister Gregor Werner. Werner was too old and weak to fulfill his duties, but he was kept on the job because to demote or simply fire him would

Prince Paul Anton Esterházy was the head of the richest family in Hungary. His sponsorship of Haydn in 1761 was vital to the composer's career.

have been unthinkable, even for a family as powerful as the Esterházys. So Haydn was brought in to work as acting kapellmeister, with the title of vice kapellmeister and the understanding that he would take the post when Werner died. As such, he was answerable to Werner regarding choir music.

In 1765, Werner wrote a vicious letter of complaint to Prince Nicolaus Esterházy (1714–1790), who succeeded his brother Prince Paul Anton to the throne in 1762, about Haydn's supposedly neglectful management. It read, in part, as quoted in *Haydn, His Life and Music* by H. C. Robbins Landon and David Wyn Jones:

> *I am forced to draw attention to the gross negligence in the local castle chapel, the unnecessarily large princely expenses, and the lazy idleness of the whole band, the principal responsibility for which*

must be laid at the door of the present director, who lets them all get away with everything, so as to receive the name of a good Heyden [sic]. For as God is my witness, things are much more disorderly than if the 7 children were about; it seems that there are only libertines among the chorus people, who according to their fancy take their recreation for five or even six weeks at a time: the poor chapel thus has only five or six at a pinch, also not one of them pays attention to what his neighbor is playing.

Werner also complained about missing instruments and disorganized sheet music. There seems to be a good chance that many of Werner's complaints may have been justified, as Haydn had an easygoing reputation, and he found administrative work boring in contrast to the joy of writing and performing music.

Prince Nicolaus sent Haydn a seven-point directive dealing with the complaints, and advising the composer to become more productive. Haydn, in response, started cataloging his work to prove his value as an employee. The resulting document, the "Entwurf-Katalog" (draft catalog), was essentially Haydn's attempt to show that he wasn't slacking off at work, but it has become an invaluable resource for historians and musicians authenticating Haydn's music.

Werner died in the spring of 1766, and Haydn became kapellmeister. The job was challenging. It required a diplomat's touch to serve as a buffer between the prince and his administration and the often temperamental musicians. Much of the work was administrative, rather than musical. But Haydn soon got the hang of it. He had

a warm personality and a knack for surviving the plotting and backstabbing that was common in royal courts.

The benefits of his new position were considerable: a good salary, his own staff of servants, and living quarters most of the year at Esterháza, the newly built family palace. Completed at a colossal cost in 1766, Esterháza was the greatest castle in Europe after Versailles in France. Rising majestically from a Hungarian swamp, the fairy-tale palace sprawled out over 126 rooms on three stories. It included a Chinese-style pavilion, a coffee house, a rose garden, a small zoo, a 400-seat theater for opera, a grotto-like marionette theater, and a hunting lodge known as Monbijou. German comedies and Italian opera alternated from day to day at the opera house. Esterháza's many performance spaces provided a unique musical opportunity, as did the orchestra. (With between twenty and twenty-three musicians, the orchestra was one of the largest and best in Europe.)

A GREAT PLACE TO WORK

In 1776, Empress Maria Theresa, ruler of the Habsburg Empire, paid a visit to Esterháza. She was impressed by the splendor of the castle and by Haydn, thinking him a great musician and director. Exposure to powerful patrons, such as Empress Maria Theresa, was good, but the relative remoteness of Esterháza was even better. Located fifty-three miles (eighty-five kilometers) southeast of Vienna in present-day Hungary, the palace's remote location kept Haydn out of the Vienna music scene, forcing him to develop an original voice. As Haydn told his biographer G. A. Griesinger, as quoted by Landon and Jones, "I was set apart from the world, there was nobody . . . to confuse and annoy me in my course, and so I had to become original."

Griesinger also wrote of how Esterháza provided Haydn with the opportunity to hunt, a much-needed outlet for relaxation. He sums up Haydn's time at Esterháza as follows:

> *Hunting and fishing were Haydn's favorite pastimes during his sojourn in Hungary, and he could never forget that once he brought down, with a single shot, three hazel-hens, which arrived on the table of the Empress Maria Theresa. Another time he aimed at a hare but only shot off its tail, but the same shot killed a pheasant that happened to be*

nearby; while his dog, chasing the hare, strangled itself in a snare.

Prince Nicolaus Esterházy was an educated connoisseur and passionate lover of music, and also a good violin player . . . Haydn had his hands full; he composed, he had to conduct all the music, help with the rehearsals, give lessons and even tune his own piano in the orchestra. He often wondered how it had been possible to compose as much as he did when he was forced to lose so many hours in purely mechanical tasks.

There is no doubt that Esterháza was a wonderful setting for making music; and Haydn's success stems, in part, from Prince Nicolaus's appreciation for new music. It was also the product of the creative pressures that the composer was under at Esterháza. Haydn's life there was a whirlwind of deadlines, projects, and princely demands. He supplied music for two weekly concerts (on Tuesdays and Saturdays), from two to four o'clock in the afternoon. In 1786, for example, there were seventeen different operas given at Esterháza, for a total of 125 performances. H. C. Robbins Landon, a Haydn expert, estimated that between 1780 and 1790, Haydn conducted 1,026 performances of Italian operas alone.

Although the work was demanding, Haydn's relationship with Prince Nicolaus, who ruled until 1790, was warm. Prince Nicolaus was extremely musical, and he took great personal interest in Haydn's work.

"My Prince was always satisfied with my works," Haydn wrote, as quoted by Landon and Jones. "I not only had the encouragement of constant approval but as conductor of an orchestra I could make experiments, observe what produced an effect and what weakened it, and . . . improve, alter, make additions or omissions, and be as bold as I pleased."

THE PRINCE AND THE BARYTON

Prince Nicolaus was more than just a boss. He was also Haydn's partner as the composer made musical history. For an artist to survive, he or she needs a job. But a job takes time and energy, and by the time the artist is ready to work on composing or performing at the end of the day, he or she is already exhausted from the effort of a day's work. In order to thrive and achieve his or her potential, an artist needs a job that allows for creativity and offers time to work on great projects within his or her chosen forms.

Haydn's position with the Esterházys offered exactly this, and Prince Nicolaus's keen interest in music meant that Haydn's more creative work was very much appreciated and supported. It was Haydn's job to be a great and creative composer. This was not something that he had to shoehorn into the corners of his day, after he was done teaching or copying music for the benefit of other people.

Haydn had the freedom to write the kind of music that most excited him, but he kept in mind that Prince Nicolaus loved playing the baryton (an old-fashioned instrument that resembles the modern-day cello, but with more strings). It had six or seven bowed strings of gut, plus between nine and twenty-four "sympathetic" wire strings. These sympathetic strings weren't played with a bow or plucked; they resonated naturally when the gut strings were played. Haydn carefully looked after the

prince's interest in the instrument, writing 175 compositions for the baryton in the 1760s and 1770s. Most of these
works were trios for viola, cello, and baryton.

Prince Nicolaus's interest in comic opera also had a
major influence on Haydn's efforts. Between 1772 and
1781, most of Haydn's output consisted of comic operas.
The genre was hardly Haydn's strength, and his comic
operas are not what he is remembered for today. But
these operas had an impact on his other works. He
injected comic opera's energy, continuity, and rhythmic
timing into his later works, starting in 1781 with String
Quartets, opus 33, nicknamed *Gli Scherzi*—literally Italian
for "the jokes."

Most pieces of classical music consist of movements,
or sections of music, each with its own feel and style of
composition. In the Scherzi quartets, Haydn substituted
scherzos (a light, lively, surprising musical movement)
for the more traditional minuet movements (which tended
to be slow, ceremonious, and graceful). This was a major
development for the quartet form.

PUBLIC LISTENERS AND PRIVATE PATRONS

Every composer writes for a number of audiences (as did
Joseph Haydn in his time). He or she writes for pleasure,
trying to create a work that is challenging or beautiful for
its own sake. The composer is often trying to please his or
her boss as well. That boss may be a member of royalty
like Prince Nicolaus, or a concert promoter, or a modern-
day record producer. The composer is also trying to please
listeners and critics, who will attend concerts, buy sheet
music and recordings, and write books and articles about
the works they've heard.

The Four Princes

Over the course of his career, Haydn worked for four Esterházy princes. Each had his own style, and that, in turn, had an impact on the kind of freedom Haydn had as a composer.)

Prince Paul Anton (1711–1762): A soldier who reached the high rank of field marshall, Prince Paul Anton initially hired Haydn. Like his younger brother Nicolaus, he was an accomplished musician, and he was fond of playing the violin, flute, and lute.

Prince Nicolaus "the Magnificent" (1714–1790): A decorated soldier and Haydn's main patron and supporter, Prince Nicolaus was one of the most successful and long-reigning heads of the Esterházy family. A musician in his own right, Nicolaus played the cello, the viola da gamba, and the baryton. He often played the baryton in trios with Haydn (who, historians think, played viola). This sort of intimate music-making helped make his support of Haydn deep and understanding.

Nicolaus built Esterháza, expanded the family fortune and influence, and built upon his brother Paul Anton's already generous sponsorship of the musical arts. He was the primary sponsor of Haydn's symphonies—he made sure the composer had ample rehearsal time, full artistic control, and salary levels sufficient to tempt the top talent in Europe.

When his wife died in 1790, Nicolaus slipped into a deep sadness, and Haydn found himself struggling to comfort the prince with music during the short period of time that the prince survived his wife.

Prince Anton (1738–1794): Unlike his father, Prince Nicolaus, Prince Anton had little interest in the musical arts. In fact, in 1790, during his short reign he disbanded the Esterházy family's musicians. He gave Haydn a lifetime annual pension of 1,000 gulden (roughly 45,000 of today's dollars), and gave pensions of 400 and 300 gulden, respectively, to Luigi Tomasini (the concertmaster) and Leopold Dichtler (a long-serving tenor singer). Esterháza went from being a cultural jewel to a supersize hunting lodge, home to the occasional house party and little more.

Prince Nicolaus II (1765–1833): The son of Anton, Nicolaus II served as an officer in the empire's guards, and, later, as an imperial diplomat. He was a collector of artwork, but spent such enormous sums of money on them that he caused serious financial problems for the family's next two generations. He was, however, more interested in music than his father. He played clarinet and commissioned six Masses from Haydn.

Sometimes these forces work in opposition to one another. A boss with poor judgment, for example, can persuade a composer to write music that doesn't meet the musician's own standards of quality. An interest in pleasing crowds (or obtaining the money that the audience pays for concert tickets) can lead musicians to compose music that satisfies popular tastes, but is shallow and hollow, or perhaps steals shamelessly from successful music that has come before it.

Haydn's situation at Esterháza presented few such conflicts. While his music was shaped by the various Esterházy princes, it was rarely, if ever, distorted or cheapened by their interests. At the same time, there is a distinction between the intended audiences for different types of Haydn compositions. His symphonies speak to the listener, not the player. In contrast, his quartets and trios, while pleasant to listen to, challenged and flattered particular players that Haydn dealt with on a daily basis.

Indeed, in the small musical world within the Esterházy court, relationships sometimes lasted for decades. For Haydn, keeping his fellow musicians happy was often as important as entertaining his listeners— especially considering that one of those musicians was the wealthy and powerful prince.

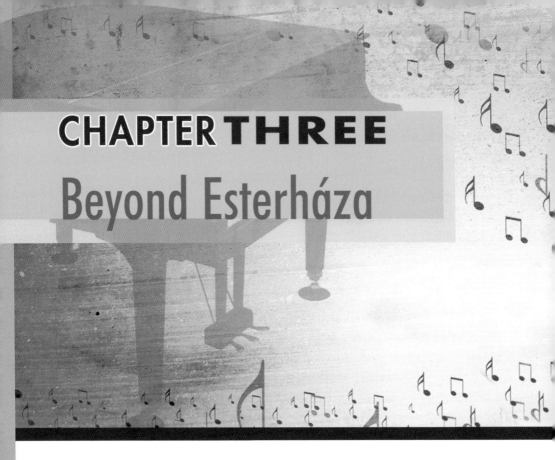

CHAPTER THREE

Beyond Esterháza

When Prince Nicolaus Esterházy died in 1790, Haydn, cut free from his longtime patron, went back to Vienna where he took a room in the house of a friend, J. N. Hamberger. After turning down several job offers, Haydn received a surprising visit from a man named Johann Peter Salomon.

Salomon was born in Bonn, Germany, but he lived in London, where he worked as a violinist and music promoter. He knew that Londoners had a hunger for Haydn's music, and had a feeling that the newly available conductor would go over fantastically with English crowds. Turning up on Haydn's doorstep, he offered to take the composer on a professional tour of London and sought to draw up a contract outlining a schedule and rates.

The contract worked out for the 1791 season guaranteed Haydn £300 for an opera, £300 for six symphonies, £200 for the rights to publish the latter, £200 for twenty other compositions to be conducted at concerts, and £200 profit from a benefit concert. Added together, this was a total of £1200 (roughly $80,500 in today's currency). This was a handsome sum for a tour that promised all sorts of additional concert and moneymaking opportunities.

THE TWO TRIPS TO LONDON

According to a letter quoted by Landon and Jones, Haydn wrote to a friend about his trip across the English Channel in 1791. He wrote, "I've stayed on deck during the entire crossing so as to gaze [at] that great monster, the ocean." London was ready for him. He went on:

My arrival caused a great sensation . . . I went the rounds of all the newspapers for three successive days. Everyone wants to know me . . . If I wanted, I could dine out every day; but first I must consider my health, and second my work. Except for the nobility, I admit no callers until 2 o'clock.

Haydn's time in London was bustling—the popular composer was deluged with royal invitations and a constant stream of visitors. It was also incredibly lucrative. His benefit concert alone, which was supposed to generate about £200, brought in £350 and enthusiastic reviews from newspaper critics. According to Landon and Jones, one critic wrote:

Never, perhaps, was there a richer musical treat. Is it not wonderful that to souls capable of being touched by music, HAYDN should be an object of homage, and even of idolatry; for like our own SHAKSPEARE he moves and governs the passions at will.

During two trips to London (1791–1792 and 1794–1795), Haydn was active as a composer. He wrote a large number of pieces, including a dozen symphonies that would collectively become known as the London Symphonies.

The London Symphonies

Much treasured by listeners, the London Symphonies (nos. 93 through 104) are the last twelve that Haydn wrote. Many regard them as the summit of his career. Symphony no. 94 in G Major has always been one of

Haydn's most popular works. Its nickname, the *Surprise Symphony*, comes from its second movement. The music starts out quietly and restfully. Soon, however, the concert hall is jolted by a very loud and unexpected chord designed to shock dozing Londoners out of their chairs. After the chord, the music immediately quiets down again.

Symphony no. 96 was nicknamed the *Miracle Symphony*. According to one story, a chandelier fell from the ceiling of the concert hall during its premiere. The audience managed to escape the chandelier unharmed, giving the symphony its name. (More recent research suggests that this event actually took place during the premiere of his Symphony no. 102.)

The tour of London was a grand triumph for Haydn. When he returned to Vienna for a final time in 1795, he was hailed as a conquering cultural hero. His fame in London had made him a musical giant in the German-speaking world.

THE CREATION

Perhaps the greatest fruit from Haydn's visits to England was the mammoth oratorio *The Creation*, which many consider to be his greatest single work. Haydn was inspired by performances of George Frideric Handel's oratorios by enormous groups of musicians in England. Upon his return to Vienna, Haydn set out to accomplish work of similar weight using the style he had developed after a lifetime of composing.

The result is a brilliant musical celebration of one of the Bible's most well-known stories (the creation of the world by God), as outlined in Genesis, along with elements from John Milton's (1608–1674) *Paradise Lost*.

The Creation breaks into three major sections. The first celebrates the creation of the primal light, Earth, the heavenly bodies, bodies of water, weather, and plant life. The second part describes the creation of sea creatures, birds, animals, and people. The third part is set in the garden of Eden, and describes Adam and Eve before the Fall.

The oratorio opens with an overture entitled "Chaos," representing the disorder that existed before God created and organized the universe. Gradually, individual instruments pick their way out of the initial musical mess, establishing themselves as order reigns over confusion. Harmony is established, and the discordances settle, yielding to a sort of misty-sounding effect that illustrates the Biblical idea of "the Spirit of God moving upon the Face of the Waters." Then, as the music indicates God saying "Let there be light!" the whole orchestra and chorus responds in rousing song, "And there was light!" The Creation continues along these lines, both a re-imagination and celebration of something deeply Christian and spiritual.

The oratorio's scope was epic to the point of exhausting Haydn as he worked on it from October 1796 through April 1798. Indeed, he fell ill after he conducted its premiere performance at the Burgtheater in Vienna, in March 1799. The work is still widely performed and recorded today. A typical performance clocks in at one hour and forty-five minutes.

THE SEASONS

The great success of The Creation led Haydn to undertake the last epic work of his life, The Seasons (1801). An oratorio with themes as ordinary and earthbound as The Creation was extraordinary and godly, *The Seasons* explores everyday life among rural people and seasonal changes of weather.

The work is filled with "tone painting," a musical format that uses the sound of instruments to paint musical "pictures" that an audience can "see" as the notes are played. A plowman, for example, is portrayed whistling while he works. In a typically clever twist, Haydn depicts him as whistling the theme from his own *Surprise Symphony*.

Although the work is ambitious (it follows the progression of all four seasons), it lacked the emotional and religious punch of *The Creation*. As a result, even though the music is widely regarded as excellent, it met a more lackluster response from the public. In the wake of the muted reception *The Seasons* received, Haydn complained about the libretto, which was written by the Austrian baron Gottfried van Swieten. He didn't mince his words—he referred to it as "French trash" to his friends.

FINAL DAYS

By the beginning of the nineteenth century, the sixty-eight-year-old Haydn was beginning to fade. Still actively consulting and teaching younger musicians (including Ludwig van Beethoven), Haydn gave his last public performance on December 26, 1803, when he conducted *The Seven Last Words of the Savior on the Cross*. After 1805, he wrote no letters with his own hand.

Although Haydn was celebrated throughout Europe and admired by musicians and music listeners alike, his last years had an aura of sadness about them. In *The Classical Style*, Charles Rosen wrote:

The last years of Haydn's life, with all his success, comfort and celebrity, are among the saddest in music. More moving than the false pathos of a pauper's grave for Mozart . . . is the figure of Haydn filled with musical ideas which were struggling to escape, as he himself said; he was too old and weak to go to the piano and submit to the discipline of working them out.

War between Austria and France hastened Haydn's decline. On May 11 and 12, 1809, French troops bombarded Vienna. Johann Elssler, Haydn's chief music copyist and friend, wrote an account of the attack in a letter to Griesinger. According to Landon and Jones, after cannon fire landed close enough to shake the windows and blow open a door, Haydn consoled his terrified servants, saying, "Don't be frightened, children, for where Haydn is no harm can come to you." Despite Haydn's passionate patriotism toward Austria, the French respected him as a great composer and cultural treasure. During this period, a French officer visited Haydn at his home, and sang an aria from *The Creation* in the composer's honor.

On May 26, 1809, Haydn played his last piece of music. Landon and Jones say that according to Elssler, Haydn sat at his piano and played "God Save Franz the Emperor," a patriotic song that he wrote in 1787, "with such expression and taste that [he] was astonished about it himself . . . and was very pleased." He had to be assisted to bed after that, and he never rose again. At about twenty minutes before one o'clock in the morning on May 31, he died. Because of the surrounding war, only a simple burial service was possible. It took place the next afternoon.

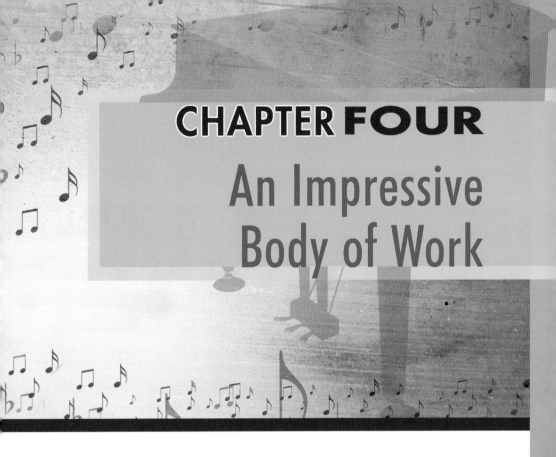

CHAPTER **FOUR**

An Impressive Body of Work

The story of Haydn's musical career is one of slow gains and careful consolidation. Although he had plenty of flashes of genius, had Haydn died at age thirty-five (six years into his career at Esterháza) he would be mostly forgotten today.

Haydn's time at the Esterházy court was the first major building block of his career. That he was able to move from obscurity to success as a court-sponsored musician isn't so unusual. Many artists have overcome challenging childhoods to achieve comfortable situations later in life. But that he managed to defy the laziness, arrogance, and creative stagnation so typical of artists who "have it made" in order to produce more than 750

Many of Haydn's symphonies and other works of music made their debuts at this concert hall at Esterháza.

compositions, many of which are still in active circulation, is amazing.

Haydn's hunger to create and to improve himself as a craftsman is a thread that runs throughout his life. As we have seen, Haydn continued to produce superb compositions after leaving the cushy confines of Esterháza. In contrast to Mozart, who stormed the world with the speed and flash of a lightning bolt, Haydn built slowly over his long life, increasing his gains as an artist and growing stronger and better as the years went by.

The String Quartets

Haydn wrote sixty-eight string quartets and was an acknowledged master of the form. As the name suggests,

Haydn is often referred to as "the father of the string quartet." This painting shows him playing in a string quartet at Esterháza.

string quartets are comprised of four stringed instruments. In modern times, this usually means two violins, a viola, and a cello, but in Haydn's day, other string instruments were sometimes used.

Quartets have their roots in the Baroque "suite" form. Haydn's Opus 9 Quartets of 1769 to 1770 modernized the suite, transforming it into the quartet as we know it. Haydn's new quartet consisted of four movements: a fast movement, a slow movement, a minuet and trio, and a fast finale. Because Haydn helped establish the style definitively, he is often called "the father of the string quartet."

Writers have commented on the way Haydn's quartets have an aura of conversation about them—the instruments seem to be talking, joking around, arguing with one another, or cutting one another off. Comic interruptions and social dynamics as complicated as a spoken discussion distinguish Haydn's most sensitive quartets as among his best work.

SYMPHONIES

Even without his 108 symphonies, Haydn would still be a great and prolific composer. But it was through these extended works that he stamped his name into the history books as the ultimate example of classical musicianship and "the father of the symphony." This title is a little controversial. Some critics give Haydn most of the credit for establishing the modern symphony format. Others think that is overly generous. But all agree that his many symphonies and great efforts to refine the format had enormous influence in the years to come.

Haydn's service with the Esterházys gave him the chance to experiment with the composition of symphonies. He wrote about twenty-five during his term as vice kapellmeister alone (1761–1766). During his early years with the court, he produced his first great works in the form: Symphonies no. 6 (*The Morning*), no. 7 (*The Afternoon*), and no. 8 (*The Night*).

Some of Haydn's greatest symphonies were composed near the end of his life. His Paris and London series of symphonies remain popular to this day. Haydn wrote the Paris Symphonies (nos. 82 through 87) in 1785 and 1786. They were commissioned by a Parisian orchestral society and written for performances in France in 1787. While not as highly regarded as his London Symphonies, the Paris Symphonies are much praised for their lively, unpredictable nature and are sometimes known by playful nicknames (no. 82 is *The Bear*, no. 83 is *The Hen*, and no. 85 is *The Queen*). The London Symphonies were a particular feather in his cap, as he had the chance to conduct them for rapturous, adoring audiences.

OPERAS

Although Haydn spent much time at Esterháza conducting and directing operas, he never quite nailed the format. He wrote thirteen Italian operas, four Italian comedies (which used spoken dialogue), five or six German singspiels (similar to opera, but with more spoken dialogue and folk-like songs), and some incidental music for plays. They were largely forgotten after his death, fading compared to the brilliance of contemporaries such as Mozart, whose *Marriage of Figaro* and *The Magic Flute* remain popular. *Orlando Paladino* (1773) was Haydn's most famous opera during his lifetime.

In general, Haydn's operas suffered from comparatively weak librettos—the characters often lacked plausibility or motivation—as well as overly formulaic and repetitive music. However, his work on comic operas is seen as a liberating influence on the rest of his musical composition—particularly on his later symphonies, which were often witty and eccentric.

ORATORIOS AND MASSES

Remembered today for his symphonies and quartets, Haydn was also a prolific composer of vocal music, most notably *The Creation*. It accounts for about half of his total output.

There are just fourteen Haydn Mass settings, starting with early work that is mostly regarded as run-of-the-mill and building to his six late Masses, most notably the

"Coronation" Mass and the "Harmony" Mass. These latter pieces are renowned as masterworks in their own right. The composer exploits the interplay between the chorus and soloists with a great deal of freedom, making for music that is challenging and original.

PIANO SONATAS

Haydn brought a new sense of order and formality to the piano sonata form. The first movement of a sonata is divided into three sections: exposition (defining the themes), development (extending the themes into new musical territory), and recapitulation (repeating and summarizing the themes). The exposition section, wherein the sonata's themes are defined, is split into two: there is a group of strong (once called masculine) themes, and a more lyric group of contrasting so-called feminine themes.

Although Haydn invented none of the format, he did more than any other composer to refine and define it for future composers. Even as he laid down the rules for sonatas with more precision than others had before him, he was dazzlingly creative within those clarified boundaries.

While Mozart's sonatas were concerned with obtaining perfect symmetry with multiple themes, Haydn was interested in the use of disparate and surprising elements to provoke his listeners with a minimum number of themes.

OTHER WORKS

In addition to his major works, Haydn composed quintets and sextets, twenty-one string trios, piano quartet-divertimentos, and a host of other incidental pieces. He also composed a number of piano trios, performed together with cello and violin (but dominated by the piano). Underpraised and little known, these compositions are regarded by a handful of critics as being among Haydn's best. The "Gypsy Rondo" Trio and the Trio in C Minor no. 13 are both considered classics within the form.

A MUSICAL SENSE OF HUMOR

Among classical composers, Haydn has always been known as the clown prince of musical humor. Musical humor, unlike verbal or physical humor, doesn't involve wordplay or a cake in the face. But it does share a key component with both: the recognition and defiance of shared expectations.

We're familiar with this pattern in verbal humor. Take the following joke, for example:

> First person: "What word is always pronounced wrong?"
> Second person: "I don't know. What word is always pro-
>   nounced wrong?"
> First person: "Wrong!"

The humor is derived from the establishment and defiance of an expectation. By asking the question, "What word is always pronounced wrong?" the questioner sets up the expectation that there's some puzzling or obscure word that is basically impossible to pronounce. The victim of the joke thinks for a while, trying to see if he or she can come up with the answer. But the expectation was false—the answer was something unexpectedly simple.

Musical humor does much the same thing. The composition leads listeners down one path, and then fails to fulfill their expectations. There's a willful playing around that makes it entertaining to experienced listeners.

Haydn's Symphony no. 92 in G Major is called the *Oxford Symphony* because he performed it at Oxford University when he received a honorary degree there. Its minuet section keeps listeners utterly baffled. It is impossible for a listener to guess where the first beat is at the beginning, and by the time the listener has begun to figure things out, Haydn introduces pauses long enough to throw him or her off again. Charles Rosen, in *The Classical Style*, called it "the greatest of all practical jokes in music."

More famously, Haydn designed the *Surprise Symphony* after he heard stories of London concertgoers' tendencies to nap during quiet songs. Its second movement is as peaceful as can be, and then suddenly, he unleashes a fortissimo, or very loud, chord designed to ambush and startle anyone who might have drifted off.

Haydn's humor is notable for being witty but essentially kind. He shares victimless jokes with his listeners, whereas other composers, such as Mozart, used musical jokes to ridicule weak musicians. In fact, it's hard to find any critical writing about Haydn that doesn't mention his sense of wit, liveliness, and fun. A major part of the composer's time was dedicated to creating works that had a sense of joy, as well as a sense of musical inventiveness. "Since God has given me a cheerful heart," Haydn wrote in his autobiography, "He will forgive me for serving him cheerfully."

CHAPTER FIVE
The Evolution of Haydn's Style

From early on in his development as a composer, Haydn liked disruptive and shocking effects. He was a master of surprise modulation, dramatic silence, and asymmetrical phrases. This sort of "shock" is normally associated with younger, less mature musicians, but Haydn's last works have more substantial shocks and changes than his earliest ones. Some of his final compositions feature musical practical jokes and daring juxtapositions of remote keys.

What changed, however, was Haydn's ability to organize his eccentric tricks and humor into the confines of a greater work. As he got older, he got better at using musical symmetry to put even the most outlandish flourish into a greater context. He gained an increasing amount of respect for the integrity of any given work—its "voice," its

An eighteenth-century portrait of Haydn at work. His time in the countryside, the creative freedom offered by his sponsors, and decades of hard work all contributed to his distinctive musical voice.

themes, its style—and he made sure all his imaginative tangents were rallied behind the big ideas that fueled the music.

Haydn's career was a long musical journey. He began as an artist within the traditional patronage system of the late-Austrian Baroque period. He ended it as a "free" artist just as Romanticism—which would make the nineteenth century so indelible—was bursting upon the scene. But throughout, he aggressively maintained his own style— borrowing at times, and taking inspiration from his childhood roots, but developing a unique voice that was echoed much more than it echoed the voices that came before it.

There are many ways to break up Haydn's career and style into periods or chapters, but none are necessarily "right." One theory looks at his life as a three-stage journey. The first was immaturity, the period when

Haydn composed within existing styles. The second, begun in earnest at Esterháza, was the experimentation phase, as he searched for a new way to compose that expressed his own ideals. The final was full maturity, as he composed his Paris and London Symphonies, the ideal for many people of what full-blown classical music really is.

Another view of Haydn's style shows that he reached a first peak around 1770, with his Sturm und Drang (storm and stress—intense, passionate, turbulent, explosive music) period, and another one with the more refined and elegant Paris Symphonies and the *Seven Last Words of the Savior on the Cross*.

However one analyzes the various periods of Haydn's career, the evolution in his style clearly reflects changes in Europe. Haydn lived through a turbulent period in European history that included the continuing retreat of religion from its dominant role in society, the Enlightenment movement, and a rise in nationalism. Moreover, the arts transitioned from the Baroque to the Classical movement and, toward the end of his life, to Romanticism.

RELIGION AND MUSIC

Haydn's composing was done at a time when music, like so much else, was moving out of the sphere of religion and into the public sphere (or into the hands of wealthy patrons). But when Haydn got his start, religion was still regarded as the wellspring of music. His first real position, as an eight-year-old cathedral choirboy, was completely defined by a respect for God and the church that would always be a critical part of his personality. Throughout his life, he was a devout Catholic, and inscribed most of his compositions "In nomine Domini" (In the name of God) at the top and "Laus Deo" (Praise be to God) at the bottom.

Although the Esterházys hired him in part because of his dedication to religion (and the serious, reliable mind-set that this represented), the emphasis on religion decreased over the course of his employment there. Religious music was not a major priority for Prince Nicolaus, and Haydn put less and less emphasis on it as the years went by.

Still, much of Haydn's work was more explicitly religious; vocal music makes up half of his output, and much of that was religious in nature. His first and last completed works were Mass settings. In addition to *The Creation*, *The Seven Last Words of the Savior on the Cross* ranks among Haydn's most explicitly and intensely religious compositions.

THE SEVEN LAST WORDS OF THE SAVIOR ON THE CROSS

The Seven Last Words was commissioned by the canon of Cádiz Cathedral in Spain. The work was to be performed on Good Friday during Lent (in Catholicism, the forty days before Easter, not including Sundays) as an aid to meditation. The song's seven slow movements (adagios) are meant to directly parallel the last remarks made by Jesus Christ while being crucified on Mount Calvary.

Originally organized as an orchestral piece, *The Seven Last Words* was also rewritten as a quartet. Haydn found the commission to be a difficult one. Landon and Jones quoted Haydn as explaining to his biographer, Griesinger:

Some 15 years ago I was requested by a canon of Cádiz to compose instrumental music on the seven last words of Our Savior on the Cross. It was customary at the Cathedral of Cádiz to produce an oratorio every year during Lent, the effect of the performance being not a little enhanced by the following circumstances.

The walls, windows, and pillars of the church were hung with black cloth, and only one large lamp hanging from the center of the roof broke the solemn darkness. At midday on Good Friday, the doors were closed and the ceremony began. After a short service the bishop ascended the pulpit, pronounced the first of the seven words (or sentences) and delivered a discourse thereon.

This ended, he left the pulpit and fell to his knees before the altar. The interval was filled by music. The bishop then in like manner pronounced the second word, then the third, and so on, the orchestra following on the conclusion of each discourse. My composition was subject to these conditions, and it was no easy task to compose seven adagios lasting ten minutes each, and to succeed one another without fatiguing the listeners; indeed, I found it quite impossible to confine myself to the appointed limits.

THE TRANSITION FROM BAROQUE TO CLASSICAL

The Classical era of music that Haydn belonged to—and even exemplified, for many listeners—is sandwiched between the Baroque music of the seventeenth and early eighteenth centuries and the Romantic period that dawned at the beginning of the nineteenth century.

Classical music has its roots in the Baroque era, a period from approximately 1600 to 1750. Well-known composers within the Baroque period include Girolamo Frescobaldi (1583–1643), Arcangelo Corelli (1653–1713), Henry Purcell (1659–1695), Johann Sebastian Bach (1685–1750), George Frideric Handel (1685–1759), and Antonio Vivaldi (1678–1741). Their work established or initiated many of the forms and styles that Haydn worked within and helped perfect throughout his lifetime of composing.

In the middle of the eighteenth century, Europe began a move toward Classicism, a new style in the arts, including architecture, literature, and music. While still linked to court culture (royal courts continued to control the money), it put a new emphasis on order, clarity, and hierarchy. Brighter contrasts and simple, understandable messages were suddenly in vogue; gaudy, over-decorated anything was out. The founders of the Classical style in music are considered to be Carl Philipp Emanuel Bach (1714–1788), and Christoph Willibald Gluck (1714–1787). Haydn cites Bach as a major influence.

Composers such as Haydn helped define classical music by firmly developing and establishing forms that had been more loose and informal during the Baroque period, such as the sonata and the symphony.

While it is difficult to summarize the many shifts that took place between the Baroque and Classical forms, it's safe to say that musical ornamentation (which can be seen as complexity and "decoration" for decoration's sake) decreased, while musical clarity and organization increased. After all, the Classical era was the musical accompaniment

A nineteenth-century painting depicts a fantasy quartet performing in heaven, featuring famous composers (*from left to right*): Ludwig van Beethoven, Franz Schubert, Wolfgang Amadeus Mozart, and Joseph Haydn.

to the Enlightenment, an intellectual movement that swept eighteenth-century Europe. The Enlightenment was dedicated to the use of superior reason, science, and philosophy to organize and classify the world.

Classical music carried on the role of counterpoint (the art of combining two simultaneous musical lines) emphasized by the Baroque period but diminished it. A "gallant" homophonic style (the use of a single melodic voice and rhythmically similar accompaniment) becomes much more prevalent during the Classical period.

The changing of keys (known as modulation) also took on new importance in classical music. Modulation occurred in Baroque music but less deliberately than in classical music, where compositions are often structured as dramatic journeys through a sequence of music keys. Similarly, Baroque music tends to keep a fairly stable level of dramatic energy throughout. Classical music, on the other hand, tends to tell a more progressive story, establishing tensions and resolving them with a dramatic climax. Classical music also tends to be more emotionally complicated than its Baroque predecessor, shifting "moods" multiple times within a single movement.

The Classical era is perhaps best defined by its three leading composers: Mozart, Beethoven, and Haydn. Although the passion of Mozart, the forceful storminess of Beethoven, and the elegant good humor of Haydn are radically distinct, the composers all shared certain attitudes and stylistic flourishes typical of their era. At the same time, they all have different relationships to the period. While Haydn and Mozart helped define its Vienna school of music, Beethoven defied many of its conventions, opting for a darker and more personal approach to music that foreshadowed the Romantic period.

THE ROMANTIC PERIOD AND NATIONALISM

As Haydn's life came to close, and Beethoven came into his own as an acknowledged master of music, so did music begin to depart from the orderly forms of the Classical era. Nationalism—the organization of individual cities and powerful political dynasties into political units that resemble modern nations—was beginning to sweep Europe in earnest. Religion's retreat freed the composers of the eighteenth century, and particularly the nineteenth century, to pursue new themes.

The phrase "romantic music" conjures up soft, relaxing, mood-setting music that's perfect for a dance or a dinner at a cozy restaurant, but Romantic music was often far from that ideal. The Romantic era put a premium on longer, more dramatic pieces of music that often had nationalistic themes and blasting, passionate, intense stretches of sound that required larger orchestras armed with rarely used types of instruments. Composers moved away from the organization of the Classical era, and toward the "color" of increased musical breadth. Still, much of the era's fundamental substance was drawn from the Classical period and the forms Haydn helped establish.

Haydn's main contribution to nationalism, and one of his most popular works, is "God Save Franz the Emperor," a patriotic song that was adopted as the Austrian imperial anthem. He tellingly referred to the work as a "volkslied," which can mean either a folk song or a national song. On the emperor's birthday on February 12, 1797, Haydn's volkslied, later to be known as the imperial anthem, was heard for the first time, in the presence of the imperial couple. It was a major success.

The Pastoral Voice: Haydn and Folk Music

Haydn's enthusiasm for national ambitions was also expressed in his embrace of local music. Although he was among the most sophisticated composers of his time—or any time, for that matter—many of his works had undertones that could be described as rural, or countrified. When you consider Haydn's childhood, this isn't so unusual. Haydn's father was a skilled folk musician, who had taught himself to play the harp. According to interviews with the composer, the Haydn family frequently sang together as well as with their neighbors. This deliberate use of the simple charm of folk music is often described as a rustic or pastoral style.

Pastoral classical music composed in twenty-first-century America might have hints of square dancing—the violins might take on the sound of fiddles, a banjo might plink away as part of the orchestra, and the melodies of country-western songs might be woven into the score. Or it might reach further, beyond the rural world into the world of popular music, and incorporate riffs and hooks from genres such as hip-hop or heavy metal.

Haydn, too, made an effort to reach outside the closeted world of the court composer by using rural (and, more generally, popular) elements in his music. He took inspiration from Croatian, Austrian, and gypsy (Romany) folk songs. He hijacked the melodies and rhythms of yodelers, used bagpipe effects, and made musical allusions to specific peasant dance tunes. His use of Croatian folk songs has stoked an ongoing (and sometimes raging) debate about whether the composer himself was of Austrian or Croatian ancestry.

Although the influence of folk songs on Haydn's music is obvious, the links between actual identifiable folk songs and Haydn's music are sometimes hard to decipher. When Haydn incorporated something like a folk melody into one of his compositions, he rarely did it without making significant changes. In general, he would keep the beginning of a tune and modify the end. Sometimes the tune would be basically unaltered, but it would be given a sophisticated musical development. At other times, Haydn would change the tune around, making it more expressive. But the changes weren't made to hide the popular sound of the original melody; often, they reinforced it. Haydn had fully mastered his popular and pastoral style by 1790.

Haydn's playful use of the pastoral—combined with his upbeat, amiable style—contributed to his music losing popularity in the nineteenth century. He was soon eclipsed by Beethoven, whose music contained an aura of mystery and tension that Haydn simply didn't use. Haydn preferred a seemingly simple and cheerful mask, one that hid a voice every bit as sophisticated as Beethoven's. The naive surface innocence that Haydn adopted concealed enough tricks and brilliance to keep any avid listener happy. However, the audiences of the nineteenth century didn't want rustic wit or upbeat, cheerful music. They wanted dark, ominous music that reflected the political and artistic storms that were sweeping over Europe as revolutions forged nations from France to Germany to Italy.

CHAPTER SIX

An Enduring Legacy

Although Haydn's work lost popularity during the Romantic period, only truly being rediscovered by the public through recordings after World War II (1939–1945), his influence remained behind the scenes. He did much to shape and define the way both string quartets and sonatas are written, refining the formats' principles and influencing composers to the present day. He did much to consolidate the way symphonies are shaped and written, having written more than 100 of them himself.

Haydn developed a musical style that found a fresh balance between striking irregularity and large-scale symmetry. That is to say, his pieces had moments that were surprising, wild, or dramatic, but were well organized, carefully paced, and balanced as a whole.

This eighteenth-century painting shows Haydn *(left)* with Mozart. Mozart greatly admired and was inspired by Haydn's work, and Haydn learned much about the expressive possibilities of music from the younger composer.

Mozart und Haydn

With Quartets op. 20, he developed a texture known as classical counterpoint. It abandons the idea of equality among the instruments within a piece. In classical counterpoint, the leading "voice" or instrument moves from its position back into an accompanying role, while an accompanying voice becomes the new leader.

INFLUENCE ON MOZART

If every work that Joseph Haydn wrote was suddenly erased from our memory—every piece of sheet music burned, every CD and record smashed, every MP3 deleted—he would still be remembered for his powerful influence on Wolfgang Amadeus Mozart, one of classical music's greatest stars.

Haydn was the first composer that Mozart truly admired. The younger composer studied the six quartets of Haydn's Quartets op. 33 and used them as models for six of his own quartets, written between 1782 and 1785. "I learned from Haydn how to write quartets," he later wrote, as quoted by Harold Schonberg. "No one else can do everything, jest and shock, create laughter and profound emotion, as Haydn can, and no one can do everything as well as Haydn can."

Haydn was grateful and impressed after hearing these six quartets performed at Mozart's home in Vienna. "Before God and as an honest man," he said to Mozart's father, Leopold, "I tell you that your son is the greatest composer known to me, either in person or by name."

Mozart dedicated the quartets to Haydn with a warm note:

> *During your last stay in this capital you yourself, my very dear friend, expressed to me your approval of these compositions. Your good opinion encourages me to offer them to you and leads me to hope that you will not consider them wholly unworthy of your favor. Please then receive them kindly and be to them a father, guide, and friend! From this moment I surrender to you all my rights over them. I entreat you, however, to be indulgent to those faults which may have escaped a father's partial eye, and, in spite of them, to continue your generous friendship to one who so highly appreciates it. Meanwhile I remain with all my heart, dearest friend, your most sincere friend.*

One of Mozart's most popular compositions was greatly influenced by Haydn's Symphony no. 75. The symphony's slow movement, with its soft, hymnlike theme, is something that Haydn appears to have been the first to write. It's also a model for much of the music Mozart wrote for his two-part operatic masterpiece *The Magic Flute*.

In total, Haydn's influence on Mozart was considerable, but the influence worked in both directions. In *The Lives of Great Composers*, Harold Schonberg writes:

> From Mozart, Haydn got new ideas about organization, about key relationship, and, above all, about the expressive possibilities of music. Certain it is that after exposure to Mozart's music, Haydn's became broader than it had ever been, deeper, more expressive. It worked both ways. Mozart learned a great deal about structural organization from Haydn.

Mozart and Haydn had much in common in terms of style. In most of their works, the interplay between the tonic (the first note of a musical scale) and dominant (the fifth degree of that scale) is used as a guiding light for the composition. Both also composed pieces that tended to be fairly sunny and accessible.

INFLUENCE ON BEETHOVEN

Haydn's influence on Ludwig van Beethoven was less obvious than it was on Mozart. Though Beethoven had a few lessons with the much older Haydn, nothing much came of them. Beethoven saw himself as his own man, saying, "What is in my heart must come out and so I write it down," as quoted by Schonberg. The unspoken part of the message was, "And it doesn't matter what anyone else says about it."

In most ways, however, Beethoven's style of composing and conducting is an evolution (but not a radical break) from that of Haydn. "Much of the broadening of [Beethoven's] language and structure," wrote H. C. Robbins Landon and David Wyn Jones in *Haydn: His Life and Music*, "represents a logical development or enhancement of Haydn's own practices."

Beethoven's masterful symphony *Eroica* was influenced by a kind of dramatic musical introduction utilized in several of Haydn's quartets. Haydn's Quartet op. 71, no. 3, for example, begins as a single strong chord that is something of a false start—the music's true body (or "discourse") begins shortly afterward.

In contrast to the work of Haydn, Beethoven's pieces required much interpretation and guidance from conductors—so-called virtuoso conducting. Much of Beethoven's work was deliberately difficult, and he was perhaps the first composer to spend most of his life writing music that went out of its way to challenge both players and listeners.

Haydn and Mozart, by contrast, put together more classically beautiful and robust pieces of music that didn't require much, if any, on-the-spot fine-tuning in order to sound marvelous. This shift toward the more individually expressive virtuoso mode is part of the move from eighteenth-century classical composers such as Mozart and Haydn to the Romantic period composers of the nineteenth century. Beethoven's style is seen by some critics as a partial bridge to the Romantic era.

That said, Beethoven had a great respect for Haydn as a master of his craft and a giant among composers. In *A Creative Life in Music*, Karl Geiringer writes about a performance of Haydn's masterwork *The Creation*, in honor of the composer's seventy-sixth birthday, in 1808:

> *Beethoven stood with the members of the nobility at the door to receive "the venerable guest on his arrival there in Prince Esterházy's coach." Haydn was carried into the hall in an armchair to the sounds of trumpets and drums; Beethoven "knelt down before Haydn and fervently kissed the hands and forehead of his old teacher." After Haydn's death, Beethoven always referred to him with the greatest praise and affection, regarding him as the equal of Handel, Bach, Gluck, and Mozart.*

HADYN'S LEGACY

It's difficult to overstate the importance of Joseph Haydn in terms of the development of classical music and the Classical period. He was so productive, talented, and admired even during his lifetime that his music has had a dramatic impact on the way music has been written, played, and listened to ever since.

Haydn symbolized the virtues of the Enlightenment, the intellectual movement that dominated much of the eighteenth century (and greatly influenced the Founding Fathers, who wrote America's Constitution). His music was balanced, measured, and organized. If he lacked the dramatic passion of Mozart or the dark power of Beethoven, he made up for it with a vast quantity of music that was stirring and bright. Although nearly two centuries have passed since Haydn's death, his work lives on, vital as ever.

TIMELINE

1732	Born March 31 in Rohrau, on the west bank of the river Leitha that separated the Austrian monarchy from the kingdom of Hungary.
1740	Recruited by the kapellmeister of St. Stephen's in Vienna to sing for the cathedral choir.
1749	Haydn leaves choir school after his voice breaks, beginning a rough and impoverished period as a freelance musician.
1754–1756	Haydn serves as an extra singer for the Bohemian Court Chancellery. In 1756 and 1757, he also serves as a freelance violinist.
1757	Appointed kapellmeister to the Morzin family. He composes his first symphonies.
1760	Haydn marries Maria Anna Aloysia Apollonia Keller, daughter of a professional wig maker who employed Haydn as a music teacher.
1761–1790	Haydn comes to the Esterházy court. He begins as the assistant of Gregor Werner, the aging kapellmeister.
1762	Prince Paul Anton dies and is succeeded by Prince Nicolaus Esterházy.
1766	Werner dies. Haydn succeeds him as kapellmeister to the Esterházy court.
1766	Prince Nicolaus converts a hunting lodge into the sprawling palace of Esterháza.
1779	Haydn's contract is changed to allow him to sell and perform his music outside of the Esterházy court, turbocharging his career.

1790	Prince Nicolaus dies, and Prince Anton succeeds him. All the musicians except for Haydn and conductor Luigi Tomasini are fired.
1791	Haydn arrives in England on New Year's Day. He returns to Vienna in July 1792, heading back to London in January of 1794. He returns again to Vienna in August 1795.
1794	Prince Anton dies and is replaced by Prince Nicolaus Esterházy II, who renews musical life at the court.
1796	Haydn moves to Gumpendorf, a Vienna suburb, where he spends the rest of his life.
1798	First semipublic performance of *The Creation* oratorio.
1799	First public performance of *The Creation*.
1801	First public performance of *The Seasons*.
circa 1801	The rising profile of the Austrian national anthem "Gott Erhalte Franz Den Kaiser" ("God Save Franz the Emperor") greatly boosts Haydn's popularity.
1802	Haydn's last major work, *Harmoniemesse*.
1803	Haydn makes his last appearance in public as a conductor of his music.
1806	Haydn is housebound.
1809	Haydn's house is caught in crossfire between French and Austrian troops. Haydn dies of unrelated causes on May 31.

LIST OF
SELECTED WORKS

The Paris Symphonies: Symphony nos. 82–86 (1785–1786)

The Seven Last Words of the Savior on the Cross (1787)

The London Symphonies: Symphony nos. 93–104
  (1791–1795)

"Gott Erhalte Franz den Kaiser" ("God Save Franz the
  Emperor") (1797)

The Creation (1798)

Symphony No. 6 in D major ("Le Matin") (1761)

Symphony No. 7 in C major ("Le Midi") (1761)

Symphony No. 8 in G major ("Le Soir") (1761)

Symphony No. 22 in E flat major ("Philosopher") (1764)

Symphony No. 31 in D major ("Hornsignal") (1765)

Symphony No. 45 in F sharp minor ("Farewell") (1772)

Symphony No. 88 in G major (1787)

Symphony No. 92 in G major ("Oxford") (1789)

String Quartet No. 30 in E flat major ("The Joke") (1781)

String Quartet No. 46 in F minor ("Razor") (1788)

String Quartet No. 62 in C major ("Emperor") (1797)

Cello Concerto No. 1 in C major (1765)

Cello Concerto No. 2 in D major (1783)

Keyboard Sonata in C minor, H. 16/20 (1771)

Trumpet Concerto in E flat major (1796)

Mass No. 7 in C major (*Missa in tempore belli*, or Mass In
  Time of War) (1796)

Mass No. 12 in B flat major (*Harmoniemesse*, or Wind-band
  Mass) (1802)

The Seasons (1801)

GLOSSARY

allusion Within music, a reference to another composition; a passage of notes similar enough to the original, but re-contextualized by the new piece of music.

asymmetrical Marked by irregular beat patterns.

Baroque period A musical era from roughly 1600 to 1750, noted for its complicated, ornamented style and less formal rendering of symphonies and quartets.

baryton An old-fashioned instrument that resembles the modern-day cello, but with six or seven bowed strings of gut, plus nine to twenty-four sympathetic wire strings.

chord Three or more different notes or pitches sounding simultaneously over a period of time.

Classical period A musical era from roughly 1740 to 1830, known for its disciplined, well-organized music.

counterpoint The musical phenomenon of saying two things at once. A single "voice" added to another is called a counterpoint to that other. The more common use of the word describes that two-part combination as a whole.

discordance The quality of harmony (chords) containing sometimes unpleasant or jarring combinations of notes that convey a sense of instability.

Enlightenment An intellectual movement most prominent in Europe during the eighteenth century that moved away from religion as the source of wisdom.

It advocated reason, science, and the expansion of human arts and knowledge.

homophony Music with one prominent melodic voice and rhythmically similar accompaniment.

kapellmeister From German, literally "choirmaster" or music director for a court or cathedral's orchestra and chorus.

libretto The body of words used in a musical work such as an opera, operetta, oratorio, or musical. It typically includes both musical lyrics and spoken passages. The word itself is Italian and means "little book."

Middle Ages A period of time roughly spanning the sixth through the sixteenth century in Europe. Feudal-style rulership prevailed, as did the political and economic might of the Christian church. During this time, sacred works were the pinnacle of achievement for an artist or composer.

minuet A standard movement in the four-movement suites that evolved into the symphony. The dance that the minuet sometimes accompanied, of the same name, tended to be slow, ceremonious, and graceful.

modulation The act of changing from one key to another. Modulations create the overall structure of many pieces and add interest for listeners.

oratorio A large musical composition for orchestra, vocal soloists, and chorus. Unlike an opera, it does not have scenery, costumes, or acting.

orchestra A musical ensemble used most often in classical music. It usually consists of four sections: the strings, the woodwinds, the brass, and the percussion.

pitch The perception of a frequency of a note; highness or lowness of sound.

quartet A musical ensemble of four instruments in a string quartet, usually two violins, a viola, and a cello.

Romantic period A musical era from roughly 1815 until 1910. Musical works during this time were often long, emotionally wild, and tied to nationalistic themes.

scale A series of notes differing in pitch according to a specific scheme, which determines its quality (for example, major or minor).

scherzo A term describing a composition that is lively and surprising in its rhythmic or melodic material.

singspiel A form of German-language musical drama. Singspiel is similar to opera, but with a lot of spoken dialogue and simpler, folk-like songs.

sonata A composition for one or more solo instruments, one of which is typically a keyboard instrument. Also, the name for the usual form of its first movement.

sympathetic strings Strings on an instrument that are not actually played, but naturally resonate when other strings are played with a bow or plucked with fingers.

symphony An extended piece of music typically for orchestra and made up of several movements.

tonic The first note of a musical scale, critical to the tonal method of music composition. More generally, it's the pitch upon which all other pitches of a piece of music are centered.

trio A musical ensemble consisting of three instruments.

FOR MORE INFORMATION

Academy of Ancient Music (AAM)
10 Brookside
Cambridge CB2 1JE
United Kingdom
Web site: http://www.aam.co.uk

Handel and Haydn Society
Horticultural Hall
300 Massachusetts Avenue
Boston, MA 02115
(617) 262-1815
Web site: http://www.handelandhaydn.org

Haydn Society of Great Britain
2 Aldcliffe Mews
Lancaster, Lancashire LA1 5BT
United Kingdom
Web site: http://haydnsocietyofgb.netfirms.com

WEB SITES

Due to the changing nature of Internet links, Rosen Publishing has developed an online list of Web sites related to the subject of this book. This site is updated regularly. Please use this link to access the list:

http://www.rosenlinks.com/mth/hywo

FOR FURTHER READING

Goulding, Phil G. *Classical Music: The 50 Greatest Composers and Their 1,000 Greatest Works*. New York, NY: Ballantine Books, 1995.

Hemming, Roy. *Discovering Great Music: A New Listener's Guide to the Top Classical Composers and Their Best Recordings*. 2nd ed. New York, NY: Newmarket Press, 1994.

Hurwitz, David. *Exploring Haydn: A Listener's Guide to Music's Boldest Innovator* (Unlocking the Masters). Pompton Plains, NJ: Amadeus Press, 2005.

Kallen, Stuart A. *The History of Classical Music* (The Music Library). Farmington Hills, MI: Lucent Books, 2002.

Krull, Kathleen. *Lives of the Musicians: Good Times, Bad Times (and What the Neighbors Thought)*. San Diego, CA: Harcourt Brace & Company, 2002.

Libbey, Ted. *The NPR Listener's Encyclopedia of Classical Music*. New York, NY: Workman Publishing Company, Inc., 2006.

Reader's Digest, eds. *700 Years of Classical Treasures: The Complete History of Classical Music . . . The Composers, Their Instruments, and Works*. Pleasantville, NY: Readers Digest, 2005.

Wilson, Clive, ed. *The Kingfisher Young People's Book of Music*. New York, NY: Kingfisher Books, 1996.

Zannos, Susan. *The Life and Times of Franz Joseph Haydn* (Masters of Music). Hockessin, DE: Mitchell Lane Publishers, 2003.

BIBLIOGRAPHY

Cheslock, Louis, ed. *H. L. Mencken on Music*. New York, NY: Alfred A. Knopf, 1961.

Geiringer, Karl. *Haydn: A Creative Life in Music*. London, England: Allen & Unwin, 1947.

Holmes, John L. *Composers on Composers*. New York, NY: Greenwood Press, 1990.

Jones, David Wyn, ed. *Haydn* (Oxford Composer Companions). New York, NY: Oxford University Press, 2002.

Keller, Hans. *The Great Haydn Quartets*. New York, NY: George Braziller, 1986.

Landon, H. C. Robbins, and David Wyn Jones. *Haydn: His Life and Music*. Bloomington, IN: Indiana University Press, 1988.

Rosen, Charles. *The Classical Style: Haydn, Mozart, Beethoven*. Expanded ed. New York, NY: W. W. Norton and Company, 1997.

Schonberg, Harold C. *The Lives of Great Composers*. 3rd ed. New York, NY: W. W. Norton & Company, Inc., 1997.

Sisman, Elaine, ed. *Haydn and His World*. Princeton, NJ: Princeton University Press, 1997.

Webster, James, and Georg Feder. *The New Grove Haydn*. New York, NY: Palgrave, 2002.

Wheelock, Gretchen A. *Haydn's Ingenious Jesting with Art: Contexts of Musical Wit and Humor*. New York, NY: Schirmer Books, 1992.

INDEX

About the Author

James Norton graduated from the University of Wisconsin in 1999 with a degree in history. He is the founder and editor of *Flak Magazine* (www.flakmag.com), where he has written about books, film, and music. He is the author of *Jean Jacques Rousseau: Advocate of Government by Consent* by Rosen Publishing. He currently lives in Minneapolis, Minnesota.

Photo Credits

Cover The Art Archive/Private Collection/Eileen Tweedy; p. 4 The New York Public Library/Art Resource, NY; p. 8 Private Collection/ The Bridgeman Art Library; pp. 10, 15, 30 Erich Lessing/Art Resource, NY; pp. 13, 49 © Mary Evans Picture Library/The Image Works; p. 23 HIP/Art Resource, NY; pp. 31, 43 © Lebrect Music & Arts/The Image Works; p. 38 Scala/Art Resource, NY.

Designer: Nelson Sá; **Photo Researcher:** Amy Feinberg